LOYOLA**PRESS.**

God's Wonderful Word

A transfer sticker and coloring book

Illustrations by Emma Segal
Concept by CPH Editorial Staff

LoyolaPress.

3441 N. Ashland Avenue
Chicago, Illinois 60657
(800) 621-1008
www.loyolapress.com

God's Wonderful Word
Illustrations: Emma Segal

Originally published as *God's Wonderful Word* by Copenhagen Publishing House

Scripture quotations are from the
New Revised Standard Version Bible: Catholic Edition, copyright © 1989, 1993
National Council of the Churches of Christ in the United States of America.
Used by permission. All rights reserved worldwide.

ISBN: 978-0-8294-5119-1

Printed in China
20 21 22 23 24 25 26 27 28 29 Discovery Printing 10 9 8 7 6 5 4 3 2 1

The Concept of This Book

This book will provide you with hours of contemplation with God's Word while you color the beautiful pages and decorate them with transfer stickers.

How to Use the Transfer Stickers
You will need a pencil or a ballpoint pen to use the transfer stickers on the illustrations.

Each transfer sticker sheet contains many transfer stickers that enhance the illustrations. You can use any sticker on any page of the book. It is up to your creativity and imagination!

- Take the transfer sticker sheet out of the pocket and find the sticker you wish to transfer to either the coloring page or the illustration.

- Position the transfer sticker over the place on the page you wish it to be transferred. Then place the waxy sheet between the transfer sticker sheet and the page to protect the other stickers.

- Scribble over the entire sticker with a pencil or ballpoint pen. Be careful not to scribble or touch the other stickers on the transfer sticker sheet.

- When you have completely covered the sticker, gently lift off the sheet to see how the sticker has transferred onto the page.

In the Beginning

O Lord, how manifold are your works!
In wisdom you have made them all;
the earth is full of your creatures.

Psalms 104:24

All things came into being through him, and
without him not one thing came into being.

John 1:3

Rejoice

Let the heavens be glad, and let the earth rejoice;
let the sea roar, and all that fills it;
let the field exult, and everything in it.
Then shall all the trees of the forest sing for joy before the LORD.

Psalms 96:11–13

Let heaven and earth praise him,
the seas and everything that moves in them.

Psalms 69:34

Your Word

The grass withers, the flower fades;
but the word of our God will stand for ever.
Isaiah 40:8

Happy are those
who do not follow the advice of the wicked,
or take the path that sinners tread,
or sit in the seat of scoffers;
but their delight is in the law of the LORD,
and on his law they meditate day and night.
They are like trees
planted by streams of water,
which yield their fruit in its season,
and their leaves do not wither.
In all that they do, they prosper.
Psalms 1:1–3

My Purpose

For surely I know the plans I have for you, says the LORD, plans
for your welfare and not for harm, to give you a future with hope.

Jeremiah 29:11

Trust in the LORD with all your heart,
and do not rely on your own insight.
In all your ways acknowledge him,
and he will make straight your paths.

Proverbs 3:5-6

My Strength

I lift up my eyes to the hills—
from where will my help come?
My help comes from the LORD,
who made heaven and earth.

Psalms 121:1-2

Those who wait for the LORD
shall renew their strength,
they shall mount up with wings like eagles.
they shall run and not be weary,
they shall walk and not faint.

Isaiah 40:31

My Comfort

The LORD is my shepherd, I shall not want.
He makes me lie down in green pastures;
he leads me beside still waters;
he restores my soul.
He leads me in right paths
for his name's sake.

Even though I walk through the darkest valley,
I fear no evil;
for you are with me;
your rod and your staff—
they comfort me.
Psalms 23:1-4

Come to me, all you that are weary
and are carrying heavy burdens,
and I will give you rest.
Matthew 11:28

My Jesus

I am the vine, you are the branches.
Those who abide in me and I in them bear much fruit,
because apart from me you can do nothing.
John 15:5

I can do all things through him
who strengthens me.
Philippians 4:13

My Shepherd

I am the good shepherd.
I know my own and my own know me,
just as the Father knows me
and I know the Father.
And I lay down my life for the sheep.
John 10:14–15

All we like sheep have gone astray;
we have all turned to our own way,
and the LORD has laid on him
the iniquity of us all.
Isaiah 53:6

My Salvation

For God so loved the world that he
gave his only Son, so that everyone
who believes in him may not perish
but may have eternal life.

John 3:16

There is salvation in no one else,
for there is no other name
under heaven given among mortals
by which we must be saved.

Acts 4:12

My Hope

And I heard a loud voice from the throne saying,
"See, the home of God is among mortals.
He will dwell with them; they will be his peoples,
and God himself will be with them; he will wipe every tear from their eyes.
Death will be no more; mourning and crying and pain will be no more,
for the first things have passed away."

Revelation 21:3–4

In my Father's house there are many dwelling-places. If it were not so,
would I have told you that I go to prepare a place for you?

John 14:2